Close Fire and European Or

Wargames Rules for Miniatures

Seventeenth Century Europe

Copyright © Simon MacDowall

Revised Edition 2021

Coign Press

ISBN: 978-1-326-31340-1

All rights reserved

Introduction

Close Fire & European Order are wargames rules originally designed to re-create the battles of the early 18th Century in Europe with miniature figures. Many of the rule mechanisms were developed from Andy Callan's American War of Independence rules — *Loose Files and American Scramble*, which were published in *Wargames Illustrated # 1* (1987).

This version is an adaptation which takes the rules back in time to the era of 'pike and shot.' The main focus of the 17th Century adaptation is the Thirty Years War and the English Civil Wars. They also cover the wars of Louis XIV of France up to the end of the 1600s.

A Thirty Years War Swedish Army deployed for battle.

The historical period covered by *Close Fire XVII* is one of transition from medieval to early modern warfare — marked by the increasing ascendancy of infantry and the transition from pike to shot. For much of this period cavalry tended to rely on firepower rather than cold steel, while armour gradually gave way to buff coats.

Individual units are represented but the basic playing piece is really a *battalia* (or battle) of several units grouped together. Players will find that they need to manoeuvre each battalia as a single entity with the various units supporting each other. Deployment several lines deep will usually be much more effective than a single line. The command and control rules that encourage this are simple and subtle. Units in range of their leader will usually act as the player wishes, however, if the battalia becomes broken up then the player will lose control and units may start doing things other than what he might wish.

At the heart of the rule mechanisms is the concept of *Disorder Points* (DPs). These were invented by Andy Callan for his American War of Independence rules and have proven to be an enduring and elegant way of reflecting the variable state of morale and combat effectiveness. The system is easy to use, does not require any paperwork and dispenses with the need for lots of morale checks.

Terms with specific meanings are given in *italics* in the first instance. Their precise meaning is given in the definitions section at the end of the rules.

Additional tips and notes are delineated in this font.

Contents

Getting Started
    What you need to play   4
    Scale   5
    Troop Types   5
    Basing   7
    Units   8
    Efficiency Grades   9
    Organising the Army   9

Setting up a Game
    Attack on a Defended position   11
    Meeting Engagement   12
    Multi-player Games   12
    Umpires   12

Command and Control
    Chain of Command   13
    Command Actions   13
    Orders   14
    Control   15
    Control Test   16
    Risk to Leaders   16
    Visibility   17

Morale
    Death, Disorder and Desertion Points   18
    Removing DPs   19

Sequence of Play   20

Formations
    Line   21
    March Column   21
    Assault Column   21
    Unformed   22

Movement
    March Moves   23
    Tactical Moves   23
    Tactical Move Distances   24
    Fatigue and Disorder   25

Manoeuvre
    Wheel   26
    Formation change   26
    Re-form unformed   26
    Unlimber guns   26
    Cross obstacles   26
    About face   27
    Incline   27
    Side-step/step-back   27
    Mount/dismount   27
    Passage of lines   27
    Passing a gap   27
    Maximum DPs for movement   27

Giving Fire
    Eligibility   28
    Ranges   29
    Artillery Fire   29
    Infantry and Cavalry Fire   30

Combat & Close Fire
    Charges   31
    Charge à l'Outrance   31
    Charge Responses   32
    Combat Resolution   33
    Bases in Combat   34
    Supported   34
    Multiple Unit Combats   34
    Combat Results   35
    Actions Resulting from Combat   36

Definitions   37

Quick Reference Sheet   40

Getting Started

What You Need to Play:

Sufficient figures in your preferred scale organised into units of infantry, cavalry and artillery.

Measuring sticks or tapes to measure move distances and ranges. If using 15mm figures or smaller, these should be marked in half inch graduations (with each ½ inch representing 10 yards). If using 25-28mm figures 1 inch represents 10 yards.

Dice. Lots of normal 6-sided dice (D6), and a few average dice (AvD) marked 2-3-3-4-4-5. If you do not have AvD you can throw a D6 and count 1 as 3, and 6 as 4.

Terrain features to represent:

    hills which can have steep or gentle slopes.

    linear obstacles such as streams, hedges, ditches, fieldworks, Some, such as fordable rivers can be classified as 'major obstacles'.

    rough terrain such as woods, marshes, soft ground and towns or villages.

A tabletop or other playing surface large enough to accommodate the number of units in use. A 6 x 4 foot surface will handle most smaller games in 15mm scale but bigger surfaces are better for larger scales or bigger battles.

Suitable markers to indicate actions which would be helpful if they were visually indicated on the table. The following markers are recommended:

    Leader Markers - Individual mounted officers and command groups to indicate the location of leaders.

    Messenger Marker - a single mounted staff officer, runner, or rider to act as a messenger when changing orders.

    Inspiration Marker - dismounted officer or NCO figures in advancing or inspiring positions, placed beside a leader to show he has allocated command points to inspire a unit (see p.14).

    Horse-holder Marker - a single dismounted dragoon and one or two horses, to mark the location of horses of dismounted dragoons.

    Firing Marker - cotton wool to indicate units which have given fire.

    Disorder Markers - Units will accumulate disorder points (DPs) throughout the game. Pieces of gravel make especially good markers for this purpose since they can be more easily handled than counters and blend in well with the battlefield terrain. Alternatively, very small six-sided dice could be used.

    Fixed Bayonet Marker - a single figure with fixed bayonet to indicate troops with fixed plug bayonets.

    Halt Marker - a small counter, painted or textured to blend with the battlefield to indicate units which may not move.

    Artillery Crew Marker - a group of artillery figures to indicate the location of crews that have abandoned their guns.

Scale

The scale is not fixed however the rules have been designed with a a rough scale of one miniature figure representing approximately 50 men and one gun model representing five.

One inch on the wargames table represents 10 yards for 25-30mm figures, or 20 yards for 10-15mm scale. All measurements used in the game are given in multiples of 10 yards (1 inch in 25-28mm scale, 1/2 inch in 10-15mm scale.)

Players with 20mm figures should chose either the 15mm or 28mm ground scale and adjust the figure-man ration depending on the number of figures they mount on the bases. Those using 6mm miniatures should keep the 15mm scale but have more figures per base (see p.7).

Troop Types

Individual figures are mounted on bases of a standard size (see p.7) then organised into units of one of the following types:

Foot. Regiments of pike and shot with pike in the centre and shot split evenly on both flanks. The ratio of pike to shot may vary from 2:1 to 1:2. Some units of foot could be shot only, particularly later in the century when plug bayonets started to make pikes redundant.

A unit of French foot containing two bases of pikes in the centre and two bases of shot on either side.

Skirmishers. Men who fight in loose or dispersed formations to harass the enemy at a distance. This includes East European hajduks; Scottish archers; a forlorn hope of musketeers or arquebusiers; commanded musketeers accompanying cavalry; and dismounted dragoons.

Swordsmen. Spanish sword and buckler men, Scottish highlanders and any other infantry armed with close quarter weapons only (including halberdiers).

Cuirassiers. Heavily armoured cavalry in full or 3/4 armour. In the early part of the 17th century some still were lance armed but most tended to rely on pistols rather than cold steel.

Horse. More lightly equipped cavalry in buff coats, some of whom might also have back and breastplates. Armed with swords, pistols and often arquebuses and carbines. This includes harquebusiers, chevaux-légers, reiters and men in cuirassier regiments who have less than 3/4 armour.

Light Cavalry. Croats, Hungarians, Poles, Turks, Anglo-Scottish border reivers and similar lightly equipped irregular cavalry who fight in dispersed formations. Some might be lance-armed, others would have missile weapons including pistols, bows and javelins.

Dragoons. Mounted infantry. When dismounted they count as skirmishers.

Rabble. Armed peasants or townspeople on foot with improvised weapons.

Guns. Artillery batteries classified as one of:

> **Light guns:** saker, drake, minion, falcon, falconet and robinet. Capable of being manhandled for short distances.
>
> **Medium guns:** culverin and demi-culverin. The mainstay of field artillery.
>
> **Heavy guns:** cannon royal, cannon and demi-cannon. Heavy guns were usually only used in sieges.

Nomenclature

Foot, rabble and skirmishers (including dismounted dragoons) are collectively referred to as *infantry*.

Cuirassiers, horse, light cavalry and mounted dragoons are collectively referred to as *cavalry*.

Skirmishers and light cavalry are collectively referred to as *light troops*.

Cold Steel.

These Spanish arquebusiers rely on firepower rather than cold steel.

Most cavalry relied as much or more on pistol fire than cold steel in combat. Often they adopted deep formations with each rank firing and then retiring to allow the next to take its place and give fire in turn (*caracole*). There were, however, exceptions. The Swedes, some English Civil War Royalists, some French and many eastern cavalry charged into hand to hand combat without firing.

Cavalry that do not give fire get an extra bonus for charging *à l'outrance*, or with cold steel only. Deeper pistol firing formations can count two ranks shooting to represent the caracole. Lance-armed cavalry may never give fire and therefore always charge à l'outrance. Dragoons may never charge à l'outrance, neither may non lance-armed cuirassiers.

Units of Horse who could theoretically either charge à l'outrance or opt for pistol firing tactics may not switch back and forth between the different tactics. At the start of the game each such unit must be declared as using either 'swords' or 'pistols'. The former being allowed to charge à l'outrance but not to use their pistols, the second being allowed to give fire but not charge à l'outrance. This could be written down on the army's order of battle and does not have to be revealed to the enemy until contact is made.

Basing

Individual figures are mounted on bases of a standard size according to their fighting style. Any basing system can be used so there is no need to re-base existing figures.

If starting from scratch, the recommended base sizes for 28mm figures are:

- Foot, rabble and swordsmen: Four figures in 2 ranks or irregularly spaced on a 4cm square.
- Skirmishers: Two figures irregularly spaced on a 4 cm square.
- Cavalry: Two figures in a single rank on a 5 cm square.
- Light Guns: One model on a stand 4 cm wide, deep enough to accommodate the model.
- Medium Guns: One model on a stand 5 cm wide, deep enough to accommodate the model.
- Heavy Guns: One model on a stand 6 cm wide, deep enough to accommodate the model.
- Leaders should be based according to rank (see Command & Control p.13).

This unit of skirmishers contains 3 bases each with two figures.

Alternate basing for Light Troops. Skirmishers and light cavalry may alternatively be mounted individually. In this case 2 figures will count as a base for shooting and in combat.

Dixon 15mm English Civil War miniatures.

6-15 mm figures. A one inch square base for infantry and 1¼ inch square for cavalry works well in smaller scales.

In 15mm scale use the same number of figures per base as for 28mm miniatures. For smaller scales mount more figures per base to give the right visual effect.

Units

A unit of six Croat light cavalry on three bases.

Except for guns, bases must be organised into units. Each unit will represents a regiment or battalion of several companies, or squadrons gathered together to fight as a single entity for the duration of the battle. The minimum unit size is 2 bases, the maximum is 12.

All bases in a unit must be either cavalry or infantry and of the same grade. They will normally be the same troop type but mixed units are allowed (eg: Spanish pikemen with a rank of sword and buckler men). All bases of the unit must remain in base to base contact with each other for the duration of the game. For aesthetic purposes and to distinguish units, bases may be separated by up to 1 inch and still count as technically 'in base to base contact'.

Artillery, civilians, baggage animals and wagons are not formed into units. Instead they operate independently as individual bases.

Guns models represent a battery of 4-6 guns.

Tip. Small units offer great flexibility but will soon disintegrate once they take fire or enter into combat. Larger units are more cumbersome to manoeuvre but offer greater staying power. Units of 4-6 bases are optimal. A unit of 6 bases could therefore represent 2 paired battalions of 600 men (3 bases) each, or several squadrons of cavalry forming a large regiment or even an entire battalia. Large Spanish Tercios could be represented by a block of 4 pike bases with 4 wings each of 2 musketeers or arquebusiers.

This large unit of foot represents a Spanish tercio. It contains 4 bases of pikemen two ranks deep, with two bases of musketeers and one of arquebusiers on each side. Arquebuses were lighter than muskets and sometimes the arquebusiers might be detached to fight as skirmishers.

Efficiency Grades.

Each unit is assigned one of the efficiency grades listed below at the start of the game. These grades reflect a unit's training, morale and experience. Units during this period were very status conscious and the elite units would always receive the best recruits, training and equipment. As a result they could usually be expected to perform better on the battlefield. Exceptions are possible but generally these grades should be adhered to:

A Grade: Elite troops. There are two categories:

These aristocratic French King's Musketeers could be A2 Grade.

> **A1.** Composed entirely of highly disciplined, well trained troops with the best possible equipment, such as veterans of the English New Model Army or the best Spanish Tercios.
>
> **A2.** High status aristocratic cavalry with lots of élan but lacking the drill and discipline of A1, such as the French gendarmes or Prince Rupert's Horse.

B Grade: Professional veterans of above average quality.

C Grade: Most well, trained units with some battlefield experience and good equipment.

D Grade: Second rate or demoralised trained units, experienced militia, and irregulars.

E Grade: Inexperienced militia, rabble, and others with little or no training.

Organising the Army

A battalia of four French battalions (units) in three lines The single mounted figure represents their commander

To prepare for a game, players must organise their units into *battalia*, each led by a *commander*. A battalia must normally be either be all infantry or all cavalry, except that dragoons may be part of either an infantry or cavalry battalia and skirmishers may be part of a cavalry one. Guns may be dispersed amongst the battalia. A cavalry battalia may contain 1 unit of foot (usually skirmishers) and an infantry battalia may contain one unit of cavalry.

Each army may be subdivided into 2 or more wings, (or lines) each under the command of a *general*. A wing may contain a mix of of foot and cavalry battalia.

Setting up a Game

The most enjoyable games are usually those where a scenario has been agreed by the players, and they have a rationale for the battle and objectives for their troops.

Scenarios can be based on historical or fictional events. They could include battles between opposing forces of unequal strengths balanced by terrain favouring the weaker army or battlefield objectives that give each side a roughly equal chance of success.

A number of suitable historical scenarios are available from my website at:
www.legio-wargames.com.

The Battle of the Dunes (1658) recreated on the games table.

If time or circumstances do not permit setting up a detailed scenario, choose by mutual agreement whether the battle will be an attack on a defended position or a meeting engagement. The latter, which involves two armies deploying simultaneously and trying to destroy each other is probably the most common wargame, but historically tended to be a rather rare event.

Attack on a Defended Position.

This type of battle is brought about when one side decides that they have sufficient numbers of troops to win and the other, although outnumbered, decides that terrain or circumstances hold enough advantages to make a stand. The attacker, therefore will certainly require more troops and probably more cavalry. The defender will be able to make better use of the terrain and might have more artillery or heavier artillery, and possibly some fieldworks.

Royalist foot behind prepared positions await the Parliamentary attack in a fictitious English Civil War game.

The composition of the armies should be worked out comparatively. The attacking army should have at least as many foot as the defender and have an overall numerical advantage of at least 3:2 (counting each base equally, regardless of type). The attacker could also have more higher grade troops. The defender may opt to reduce his numbers and replace them with fieldworks, with 80 yds of fieldworks counting as a single battalion or 3 squadrons of cavalry for comparison purposes.

The table should be laid out with at least 3 terrain features and possibly a road running in the same direction as the axis of attack. There should also be something such as a bridge, ford, converging roads, or other strategic terrain feature that gives the position a logical reason for the defender to decide to hold it and the attacker to want to capture it. Terrain features can most simply be laid out by mutual consent with the defending player choosing sides. The defender then draws a sketch map of his intended deployment and may deploy anywhere on his half of the table.

Setting up a table-top battlefield with realistic terrain features, greatly enhances the visual spectacle.

Once the positions are sketched the defender deploys those troops that can be seen from the opposing table edge (see Visibility p.17). Troops that cannot be seen are not yet deployed.

11

The simplest deployment option for the attacker is to deploy his troops anywhere on his side of the table beyond 240 yds of any enemy. If more time is available, instead of deploying, he could allocate two or three entry points on his table edge (ideally roads), write down his order of march for each entry point, and have each of his units enter in march column at these points, starting on the first turn.

Which ever deployment method is used, the attacker moves first on turn one. If entering in column, movement for each unit is measured from the table edge. The defender only deploys his remaining troops if they move or fire, or if they become visible to any of the attacker's units.

Meeting Engagement.

Numbers and quality of troops in this kind of engagement should be roughly equal, with neither side having fortifications or heavy guns. The easiest method of deciding on the terrain is for one player to lay it out and the other choose which side he deploys from. Both players draw sketch maps of their initial deployment which can be anywhere on their half of the table, beyond 120 yds of the centre. Once the maps have been drawn, players deploy all their troops simultaneously.

Variations

There are numerous ways these basic scenarios can be modified. For example, rather than deploying all the troops at once, some could arrive in march column after several turns, either to reinforce a beleaguered position or, perhaps, from a flank. To make it more interesting the player expecting reinforcements might have to dice to see if they arrive, perhaps needing a 5-6 on the first attempt, increasing by 1 on each succeeding turn.

Royalist foot at a re-fight of Sedgemoor (1685). This game involved hidden movement under the cover of darkness — requiring an umpire.

Umpires.

In large games or complicated scenarios (especially if some form of hidden movement is being used) it is often useful to have someone who is not playing (or who has only a minor, static part) to act as an umpire. His job is to ensure that the game flows well and the scenario develops properly, as well as to clarify the rules and game mechanics.

Multi-player Games

Just as real life commanders have a limited span of control, players can only handle a limited number of units before a game becomes cumbersome. Once armies start to exceed 20 units on each side, turns can start to become too long and confusing. At this point it may be better better to split the army up into several wings with different players controlling each wing. The players on the same side can then concentrate only on their own troops and move simultaneously to speed things up.

Multi-player games can result in very realistic situations where parts of an army act with very little knowledge of what is going on elsewhere on the battlefield. There is also great scope to add interest to multi-player games by introducing personal victory conditions to reflect political rivalries between leaders on the same side.

Command and Control

Chain of Command

Players take the role of leaders who must make decisions that will be carried out by the battalia under their command. Each battalia must have a *leader* represented on-table. There will also be a command group representing the commanding general. These command figures should be represented as follows:

Commanders - who command a battalia. Represented on table by a single mounted officer figure;

General - A senior leader commanding a wing or the entire army. Represented on table by a command group of two or three mounted figures.

The number of figures on the command group base could equate to the number of actions the general may take (see below). Alternatively additional single figures could be added to the leader's command group to show his relative ranking.

A commander is represented on table by a single mounted figure.

Command Actions

A general's command group moves to attach to a unit in order to influence it.

Each leader must decide, in the command phase of each turn, what he will do from the command actions below. Generals may normally take two actions (may be two of the same), Commanders normally only one.

Historically exceptional leaders, may however take an additional action so that an exceptional commander could have two actions and an exceptional general three. Equally a historically inept general could have only one action rather than the usual two.

Possible command actions are:

Move up to 120 yds in the command phase. This can include attaching to, or detaching from a unit.

The leader may move again in the movement phase either independently (if detached) or with the unit to which he is attached. Attaching and detaching may only take place in the command phase.

An attached leader is bound by any combat results of the unit to which he is attached.

Issue orders or listen them, or send messenger. Only a detached general may issue new orders.

Influence the unit to which the leader is attached. This will allow him to do one of:

- **Steady Troops.** Immediately remove a disorder point (*DP* — see p.18) from the unit in the command phase. If he does this, the unit may not move or declare a charge later in the turn. A halt marker should be placed beside the unit.

- **Inspire Troops.** Increase a unit's combat effectiveness. An inspiration marker should be placed beside the command base to note that he is inspiring. A unit which is being inspired will also move faster (see move distances p.26).

An attached leader with two actions may chose to Steady or Inspire twice. This would allow him to either remove two disorder points or give a +2 in combat. He may not, however, both steady and inspire in the same turn. An exceptional general with 3 actions may not influence more than twice in the same turn. He may, however, move and attach then influence twice.

Orders

A French general issues his orders.

Each commander should have *orders* from his superior applicable for all the troops under his command. These orders are best indicated on a sketch map or orders of battle and will normally be one of the following:

1. Defend current position.

2. Advance to and defend a specific position.

1. Advance to and attack the enemy.

Orders may only be changed by the general who issued them and this may be done either by the general being in base to base contact with the subordinate or by sending a messenger who will relay the orders.

There is flexibility as to how orders are executed. For example a commander with Order #3 may choose when and how to attack and with which units. Likewise, when defending a position the commander may redeploy his units to meet the local tactical situation and attack any enemy who have taken or are threatening the position.

Units do not require individual orders. All units that are being controlled by their leader may move and act as the player wishes, within the spirit of their battalia's orders. A unit may act contrary to its orders if it has an attached general. This does not require the leader to take an 'issue orders' command action.

Control

Units that are within 60 yds of a detached leader, are considered to be *under control* and may move and act as the player wishes within the spirit of their orders. This distance is increased by an additional 40 yds for each additional action the leader has. Therefore units within 140 yds of a detached exceptional general with 3 actions will be under control. Attached leaders only exert control over the unit to which they are attached.

Units that are not under control at the end of the command phase (after all leader actions have been taken) must normally take a *Control Test* (see p.16) to determine their actions for the rest of the turn. There are, however, exceptions:

- Units with an attached leader are controlled by him and do not normally have to test.

- Units that are part of a continuous line, in base to base contact with a controlled unit of the same battalia, may conform to moves made by the controlled unit. This means if the controlled unit halts they halt, if it moves they move with it, if it charges they charge. They only need to take a control test if they wish to attempt any different actions.

- Units that form rear lines of a battalia and are within 60 yds, directly behind an under command unit of the same battalia, may also conform to moves made by the lead controlled unit as above. In this case however the rear unit does not have to charge if the lead unit charges.

These units of English and Scots are both within 60 yds of a detached leader and therefore would not need to take a control test.

All units that wish to cease rout, pursuit, or looting, or that charged and failed to make contact last turn; must take a control test even if they are under control or have an attached leader.

A small two-base unit of English horse of the 1670s with an attached leader.

Note: Any leader in the chain of command may exercise control over troops. For example a commander might use his command action to move and attach to a unit. This means the rest of his units might not be under control. However, if those units are within 100 yds of their detached general (with 2 actions), they would be considered 'under control' and would not need to take a control test.

Control Test.

Roll 1 D6

Results: Continue rout, pursuit, loot or charge on all results except 3-4. Otherwise:

- 1-2: A2 Grade repeat last move. Others halt.
- 3-4: Act as player wishes.
- 5-6: Repeat last move.

Modifiers:

+ or -1 (optional) if leader attached.

+ or -1 (optional) if A1 or B Grade.

Units with a *halt* reaction may fire and may adjust their facing or formation to face a threat. They may not otherwise move in the movement phase and may not initiate a charge. Cavalry may, however, counter-charge if charged. After combat movement is not affected.

Tip. The control test will not bother units intending to remain halted, since all possible results will keep the unit halted. Players should, however, make sure that if they wish to have a unit make a new move that they do not have to take a control test since they will only have a 2 in 6 chance of getting the desired result.

Note: Control test results override orders.

Risk to Leaders

Leaders attached to a unit are at risk if that unit takes DPs from fire or combat.

If a leader is attached to unit that takes a DP from fire or combat, he must test to see if he is also hit.

He only needs to test once for fire and once for combat regardless of the number of DPs inflicted on the unit.

To test if a leader is hit roll one D6.

1= Potential Hit.

Roll again:

1 = Killed.

2-4 = Wounded. Leaders who previously had only one action may no longer inspire or steady. A previously wounded leader is killed if wounded for a second time.

5-6 = Near miss. No effect.

Cavalry may capture an enemy leader if he is beyond 40 yds of any friendly units and they are able to move to within 20 yds of his command base.

Visibility

Leaders and troops can only react to, or shoot at, what they can see. Visibility is restricted to line of sight, normally unlimited by distance.

Hills, towns, woods and formed units block line of sight except that:

- In woods and towns or villages, visibility is limited to 40 yds.
- Units on the edge of woods and towns or villages can see out without restriction but can only be seen from 40 yds away unless they shoot. If they do shoot then they can be seen from any distance.
- Units on higher elevation can see over intervening units that did not fire last turn and that are at least 40 yds away. They may not see over woods, towns, or units that gave fire.
- Leaders, messengers, and markers do not block line of sight.
- Skirmishers only partially block line of sight. Units can see anything that is up to 40 yds beyond skirmishers.

The Dutch Blue Guard assaulting a French-held village. Visibility inside the village is limited to 40 yds. Troops on the edge of the village can see out without restriction.

Morale

Death, Disorder and Desertion Points (DPs)

During the course of the game units will accumulate death, disorder and desertion points (DPs). These are represented by placing a marker beside the unit for each DP incurred. DPs can result from movement (see p.25) manoeuvre (see pp.26-27), fire (see pp.29-30), combat (see p.35) and morale (see below).

The DPs on each unit are indicated by pebbles in this re-fight of the Battle of the Dunes.

Once a unit has accumulated as many DPs as it has bases (up to a maximum of 6). Any further DPs from fire, combat or morale (but not movement or manoeuvre) will result in a *casualty* — the removal of a base.

Once a unit has 3 DPs (for any reason) it no longer accumulates any more for movement or manoeuvre.

DPs for morale are incurred or lost in the following circumstances:

    Their general killed or routing within 120 yds = +2 DPs

    Their commander killed or routing within 120 yds = +1 DP

    Each equal or higher grade unit routing or destroyed within 120 yds = +2 DPs

    Each lower grade unit routing or destroyed within 120 yds = +1 DP

    Each equal or higher grade unit of foot retiring within 120 yds = +1 DP

    Evade a charge = 1 DP

    Ride-through enemy after combat (see p.36) = -1DP

    Advance to take the position after combat (see p.36) = -1DP

Note: Troops were highly status conscious and therefore give less regard to lower grade units. Cavalry tended to advance and retire in equal measure and so there is no morale impact for retiring cavalry.

Removing DPs

DPs can be removed when the unit *re-dresses ranks* in the morale phase. This may only be done if they did not fight a round of combat and did not take any DPs from artillery fire that turn.

The DPs that may be removed are based on the unit's efficiency grade as follows:

- A1 Grade: Remove 1 DP. One additional DP may be removed if beyond 40 yds of enemy.
- A2, B & C Grade: Remove 1 DP if stationary.
- D & E Grade: Remove 1 DP if stationary and not under fire.

To count as stationary the unit must not have moved at any time in that turn although they may have adjusted formation or facing.

Additional DPs can be immediately removed in the command phase by an attached leader if he took a 'steady troops' action. A leader may do so even if the unit is in combat, moving or under fire.

These D Grade rebel foot at a Sedgemoor re-fight are under fire and therefore may not remove DPs by re-dressing ranks even if they remained stationary.

Spanish cavalry taking fire from the guns of an off-shore ship. Units that take DPs from artillery fire may not re-dress ranks.

Sequence of Play

All actions are conducted alternately with both players completing each phase in the sequence of play before moving to the next. In an attack on a defended position, the attacker moves first on turn one. Thereafter, and in other circumstances, dice to determine who moves first by rolling one D6. Add 1 to the die roll if the army is commanded by an exceptional general whose command group is on-table.

The high score decides whether to go first or second. Once this has been resolved the players keep the same order for all phases of that turn.

All actions are carried out from right to left, except that where unit moves intersect the lead unit may move first. Unlike other phases, Combat is resolved simultaneously.

The sequence is as follows:

1. **Bombardment Phase.** Guns may fire at any targets in range or choose to withhold fire until the Close Fire Phase. Others may not shoot in this phase.

2. **Musketry Phase.** Foot with firearms may choose to give fire. If they give fire they may not move in the subsequent movement phase. Foot with plug bayonets may also fix or unfix rather than giving fire. Fixing or unfixing bayonets does not preclude subsequent movement. Troops with fixed bayonets may not give fire. Cavalry and skirmishers may not give fire in this phase.

3. **Command Phase.** Assign command actions for each leader. Move and attach or detach leaders that are taking a move action. Move messengers relaying new orders. Remove DPs from units being steadied. Once leader actions are complete, determine if any units are not under control and take required control tests.

4. **Movement Phase.** Units that are allowed to move may do so. Command bases may move freely in this phase whether or not they took a move action in the command phase. Attached leaders must move with the unit to which they are attached.

5. **Close Fire Phase.** Guns that reserved shot in the bombardment phase may give fire at close range (120 yds) but not beyond. All infantry and cavalry with firearms may shoot in this phase, even if they moved. Foot that gave fire in the first fire phase may shoot again having remained stationary in the movement phase.

6. **Combat Phase.** Declare and execute charge, counter-charge and evade moves. Simultaneously resolve combat. Conduct any moves resulting from the combat resolution.

7. **Morale Phase.** Re-dress ranks by removing DPs from eligible units (see p.19). Assign DPs for *morale*.

Notes: The effects of the bombardment phase are calculated before musketry. This gives the player moving second the possibility of reducing the capacity of his opponent's ability to shoot in the musketry phase. Withholding artillery fire allows guns to shoot at closer range on a target that may be advancing.

Tip Deciding to move first or second can make a difference which is not always immediately obvious. In some cases it is advantageous to move first since the effects of the first player's fire will reduce the second player's ability to shoot back. Moving first might also restrict the opposing player's movement options. On the other hand, moving second allows a player to wait until his opponent has moved all his troops before moving himself, thereby exploiting any weaknesses and giving his opponent no opportunity to respond to his moves.

Formations

Unit Formations

Guns and wagons operate as single models and have no formation.

Other units must normally adopt one of the two following formations:

English foot of Charles II's army in exile deployed in Line. This is the primary fighting formation.

- **Line:** This is the main fighting formation. The unit is normally in a single line with all bases side by side, in contact with each other, and facing the same general direction. A unit in line may bend its formation to conform to a terrain feature or to refuse its flank. Units may form a line several bases deep as long as the formation is at least as wide as it is deep.

- **March Column:** This is a marching formation for rapid movement not fighting. The unit is in a single file with all bases one behind the other, in contact, and facing the same direction.

- **Assault Column.** Swordsmen and foot that are assaulting fortifications, a narrow gap, or through rough terrain may also form an assault column. This is a formation which designed for hand to hand combat without giving fire. It is formed two bases wide and two or more bases deep (uneven numbers in the rearmost rank). The front two bases must have close combat weapons (swords, pikes or fixed bayonets). In case of an uneven number of bases, the smallest number should be in the rear-most rank. Troops in assault column may not give fire.

Troops in assault column attacking through rough terrain at a re-fight of the Battle of the Boyne (1690)

Unformed skirmishers in action on the flanks and in front of formed foot.

Unformed. This is the status of troops without order.

- Light troops are always unformed.
- Units that are evading, retiring, routing or pursuing, are also considered to be unformed for as long as they have that status.
- Rabble become automatically unformed whenever they move.
- Other units, or units in other circumstances, may not voluntarily become unformed.

Bases of unformed units should be spaced apart to indicate their state.

As unformed units do not attempt to maintain any order, bases are moved individually with no penalties for movement or manoeuvre. They are considered to be facing all-round with no flanks or rear.

Movement

Foot that give fire in the musketry phase may not move. Other infantry and cavalry may make either a march or tactical move in the movement phase.

Guns may move at infantry speed if limbered, as may wagons. Unlimbered medium and heavy guns may pivot up to 45° but otherwise may not move. Unlimbered light guns may make a march move at infantry speed but not a tactical move.

March Moves.

Units beyond 120 yds of enemy may make a *march move*. If making a march move, infantry, may move up to 160 yds. Cavalry may move up to 240 yds. Infantry may increase the move to 240 yds if in column on a road. Cavalry march moves are not increased on roads.

A skirmish line of dismounted dragoons engaging advancing English foot. The skirmish fire is unlikely to cause significant casualties but the presence of the dragoons within 120 yds will slow the English advance as they will no longer be able to make a march move.

Tactical Moves.

Tactical movement by units within 120 yds of enemy are determined by die rolls (see next page). When more than one die is possible the player must decide how many he will roll, then roll all at once. It is not permitted, for example, to roll one die then, after seeing the result, decide to roll another.

Units must move the full amount indicated by the dice rolled except:

- Units intending to occupy a specific piece of terrain, or to line up with other units, may halt when they reach that place. This intent must be declared in advance of rolling the move dice.

- Units must halt at 20 yds of enemy to their front. The only way to move in closer is by charging (see p.31).

- Units may halt 40 yds short if their full move would force them to interpenetrate a friendly unit or move into, or across, a terrain feature.

Tactical moves must halt at 20 yds from enemy.

All units of the same battalia that are being controlled by their commander move as a single entity using the same die roll. The same applies for units of the battalia which are not being controlled but are conforming to the movements of a controlled unit (see p.15). In other circumstances, units which are not being controlled must roll individually.

Normal moves must be in the direction of the unit's facing with no more than 22½° deviation off centre. Further direction changes will require the unit to manoeuvre (see p.26).

Tactical Move distances are as follows:

Normal Move. Infantry may move 1 AvD x 10 yds. Cavalry choose 1 or 2 AvD x 10 yards. Both may add an additional optional D6 (but see restrictions on cavalry using a 3rd die on next page). Guns may pivot but not otherwise make a tactical move.

Inspired units. Any unit with an attached leader who is inspiring adds 10 yds for every die rolled. Eg: a unit which rolls 2 dice resulting in a total of 6 on the dice moves 80 yds rather than the normal 60 yds.

Rough Terrain. Cavalry may not cross dense woods, very steep rocky hillsides, swamps, or built-up areas, unless on a road. Units moving in rough terrain are more likely to incur DPs for fatigue and disorder than in good terrain (see next page).

Moving in march column on a road negates the effect of rough terrain, including towns and villages.

Road Move. All troops may move up to 120 yds if in march column and the move begins and ends on a road. No dice required. Roads negate the effects of rough terrain.

Fast Move. Rout, pursuit evade and retire moves. The maximum possible number of dice must be used. Add 10 yds for every die rolled In an initial evade, rout or retire move, but not in succeeding ones and not if in pursuit.

Unattached Leaders & Messengers. Move up to 120 yds (240 yds if beyond 120 yds of enemy) no dice required.

24

Fatigue and disorder when moving.

There is no penalty when in march column, for unformed foot or for limbered guns. Otherwise:

- **Good terrain.** Foot and cavalry in line, incur 1 DP each time a "6" is rolled when moving in good terrain. There is no penalty if in assault column.

- **Rough terrain**. Cavalry and foot in line, incur 1 DP each time a 5-6 is rolled in rough terrain. Cavalry take an additional DP when a '4' is rolled. Foot in assault column take 1 DP on a die roll of '6' in rough terrain.

Guns may only unlimber if under control of their leader and may not limber up again. This reflects the fact that limber teams were civilians who would withdraw once the guns were placed. Unlimbered guns may pivot up to 45° but make not other tactical move. Unlimbered light guns may make a march move.

Cavalry may only change speed by up to two dice per turn. Therefore a stationary unit that decides to move may only roll a maximum of two dice for a normal tactical move. The following turn it may roll the additional optional die. Conversely a unit which moved 3 dice must move at least one the following turn unless forced to halt. A road move is considered to count as moving two dice for purposes of this rule.

Light guns may be man-handled to move up to 80 yds in a march move beyond 120 yds of enemy. Guns may not make a tactical move other than to pivot on the spot.

Unformed troops manoeuvre by each base moving freely and independently without having to maintain order. No movement penalties or DPs are incurred by unformed units for movement or manoeuvre. Unformed units are considered to be facing all-round.

This stationary cavalry unit may only move one or two AvD on its initial tactical move. If it does move then the following turn it may add the extra optional D6.

Manoeuvre

Wheel. This is the usual method of changing the direction of a unit's facing. The unit first rolls dice to determine the move distance. It then pivots on one end of the line and measures the distance moved by the outside base. If any distance remains, the unit may move forwards normally up to the full allowance.

A wheel incurs 1 DP if in line within 120 yds of enemy. No penalty if in march or assault column, or if unformed.

Formation Changes. These are done by re-arranging the unit's bases on the spot into the appropriate formation. It is possible to conduct a double formation change eg: change into column facing the flank then expand back out into line.

Formation changes take a full move and 1 DP if within 120 yds of enemy; ½ move and no DPs if further away.

Re-form Unformed Troops. The unit must first be free of whatever caused it to become unformed. This means, for example, that they have ceased pursuing or retiring. If these conditions have been met, the unit's bases may be re-arranged on the spot into either line or column, facing whichever direction the player wishes.

Reforming takes one complete move. No DPs are incurred by this action.

Unlimber Guns. This takes 1 move and 1 DP (2 DPs if under fire). Once unlimbered a gun may not limber up again.

Crossing Major Obstacles. This takes ½ move, regardless of the size of the obstacle. It causes formed units to incur 1 DP (2 if under fire). Some obstacles such as chevaux de frise which are more difficult for cavalry cause 2 DPs if cavalry cross them (3 if under fire).

Crossing Minor Obstacles. This counts as moving through rough terrain (see p.24)

Williamite troops negotiate the river obstacles at the Boyne.

About Face. This involves turning the unit around to face the rear. This is the only turn allowed by formed units. Turns to the flank are not allowed, although a unit in line could form a column facing the direction of either flank, conducting such a move as a formation change (see previous page). As unformed units are considered to face all-round they do not need to 'about face' to change direction.

> About face takes ½ move and costs 1 DP if cavalry within 120 yds of enemy or if foot under fire.

Incline. This is only allowed by A and B Grade foot in line. It is conducted as a normal move with the unit moving up to ½ its allowance to the side and an equal amount forwards. It is possible to combine an incline with forward movement. For example a unit rolling a 3 and a 4, giving it a movement allowance of 70 yds, may elect to incline 60 yds (30 sideways and 30 forwards) then move the remaining 10 yds forwards. It is not possible, however, to do this the other way around and move more to the side than forwards. No DPs are incurred for this action.

Side-step/Step-back. This is only allowed by A and B Grade foot in line. It is conducted instead of a normal move, by moving up to 20 yds back or sideways (no dice required). One or two bases of a unit may step back while the rest remain in place in order to refuse a flank. This takes 1 full move. No DPs are incurred for this action.

Mount/Dismount. Only allowed by dragoons. Replace the mounted troops by figures on foot (or visa versa). Dismounted dragoons should have a horse-holder marker placed where they dismounted to indicate the location of their mounts. Horse-holder markers may either stay in that location or withdraw up to 120 yds to a safer place. The horses may not move again on their own. In order to remount, the dragoons must be within 20 yds of the horse-holder marker.

> Mounting or dismounting takes ½ move and 1 DP if under fire.

Passage of Lines. No penalty if passing through guns. Also no penalty if none are routing and one remains stationary and did not give fire that turn. Otherwise this causes 1 DP to be incurred by each formed unit involved.

Passing a gap. Units in line wishing to pass through a gap narrower than their frontage must either:

The rear battalions of this French battalia may pass through the ones in front without penalty as long as the latter remain stationary and did not give fire.

- Reduce frontage by up to half, pass through, then expand immediately back to original formation. This incurs 1 DP if within 120 yds of enemy and reduces foot (but not cavalry) move by ½ ; or

- Change formation into march column or assault column then pass through.

Maximum DPs. Once a unit has 3 DPs for any reason it no longer incurs any more DPs for movement or manoeuvre.

Note: When ½ move is specified the unit must roll the dice then divide the total allowance by two rather than halving the number of dice being rolled.

Giving Fire

Eligibility to Fire.

Unlimbered guns, infantry, and cavalry with missile weapons may normally shoot in the the appropriate fire phases on targets to their front that are in range. Swordsmen, lance armed cavalry, pike armed foot, and foot with fixed bayonets or in assault column, may not give fire. Dragoons may only give fire if dismounted. Cavalry ordered to use cold steel only, may not give fire.

Targets must be to the firers front and within 45° of centre for formed troops or guns. Unformed troops may shoot all-round. Where several possible targets are available, each stand must fire at the nearest, except guns that are under control of their leader may choose to engage a priority target rather than the nearest one. Enemy bases within 20 yds of friends are not eligible as targets. Once a unit gives fire, a piece of cotton wool is placed in front to remind players that it fired this turn.

Caracole.

These Spanish arquebusiers deployed two ranks deep may choose to fire in caracole rather than charging.

Normally only the front rank bases of a unit may give fire. However, cuirassiers and horse two ranks deep may choose to fire in *caracole* — a formation in which successive ranks of horsemen ride up to their target, fire with pistols or arquebuses and then retire. If they choose to do this then both ranks may give fire but they may not later charge or counter-charge.

Fire and Movement. Foot that give fire in the musketry phase may not move in subsequent movement phase.

Cavalry and infantry may move and then give fire in the close fire phase. Firing does not preclude charging in the combat phase except for cavalry that gave fire in caracole or intending to charge *à l'outrance* with cold steel only (see p.31).

Bayonets. Troops with fixed bayonets may not give fire since bayonets were fitted into the musket barrels before the invention of the socket bayonet in the early 1700s. Fixing and unfixing bayonets must be done in the musketry phase instead of giving fire.

Notes: Guns that choose to reserve fire miss their chance to shoot if there is no target within 120 yds in the close fire phase.

Stationary formed foot in line potentially get to shoot twice in a turn — giving fire in the musketry phase, which then requires them to remain halted, then shooting again in the close fire phase. Cavalry, skirmishers, and foot that wish to move, may not give fire in the musketry phase but may do so in the close fire phase after completing their movement.

Ranges	Maximum Range	Effective Range	Close Range
Heavy Gun	720 yds	360 yds	120 yds
Medium or Light Gun	480 yds	240 yds	120 yds
Musketry	120 yds	-	40 yds
Cavalry*	40 yds	-	40 yds

*This includes all cavalry armed with missile weapons: pistols, arquebuses, javelins and bows.

Artillery Fire

Roll 1 D6 per gun, modified as below:

Heavy Gun	+1	Target in column, limbered or enfilade	+1
Light Gun	-1	Target in fieldworks	-1
Each DP on firing guns	-1	New target	-1
Target beyond effective range	-1	Same target and range	+1

Results:

Close Range: 2-3 = 1 DP. 4+ = 2 DPs.   Beyond close range: 4+ = 1 DP.

Artillery fire on its own is unlikely to cause significant damage but it does degrade the target's morale. A unit that takes DPs from artillery fire may not re-dress ranks in the morale phase.

Infantry and cavalry fire:

Roll 1 D6 per base able to give fire.

>Less 1 die for every DP on the unit giving fire.

>Halve dice if target is in hard cover or fieldworks. Round up in case of an uneven number.

Results:

>5-6 = 1 DP if formed foot shooting at close range.

>6 = 1 DP in all other cases.

Horse and foot exchanging fire at close range.

DPs from fire take immediate effect. Therefore DPs from previous phases and from units which fired first are taken into account when a unit gives fire.

A fire-fight between Spanish and French foot at long range.

Combat

Charges.

Hand to hand combat comes about when a unit moves into base to base contact with enemy. This is done by conducting a charge — a deliberate move into contact with the enemy with the intention of settling the issue hand to hand. It is an additional move, in the combat phase, to close the distance from up to 40 yds away.

Artillery, skirmishers and units of foot without pikes may not charge into contact unless the foot have fixed bayonets. Cavalry that gave fire in caracole may not charge. Others may charge enemy within 40 yds to their front. Enemy further than 40 yds away cannot be charged.

A battalia of horse ready to charge à l'outrance with cold steel rather than pausing to give fire.

At the start of the combat phase, each player must declare which of his units will initiate a charge. This is done in turn, starting with the player who has initiative. Players may not voluntarily cancel previously declared charges, nor add new ones, based on their opponents charge responses. To make a charge move simply move the charging unit into contact, no dice required.

Charging à l'outrance.

Charging à l'outrance (see cold steel p.6) represents a charge at the gallop with swords or lances only without pausing to fire pistols. Horse, light cavalry, and lance-armed cuirassiers may charge à l'outrance if they did not give fire. This gives them an impetus bonus in the first round of combat against other cavalry but not against infantry. A unit charging à l'outrance gets no benefit from supporting rear ranks.

Charge Responses.

Mutual Charge. Meet half way if both sides charge each other.

Stand to Receive. Units that did not themselves declare a charge will normally stand to receive an enemy charge at the halt. Move the chargers into contact.

The 'push of pike' resulting from two units of foot mutually charging each other or as one charges and the other bases to receive.

Counter-charge. Cavalry may counter-charge if charged, as long as they did not give fire in caracole. This is done by moving forwards to meet the chargers half way. Units may not counter-charge à l'outrance.

Evade. Unformed cavalry, mounted dragoons and skirmishers have the option of making an unformed fast move (+10 yds per die rolled) away from the chargers to evade contact. This costs them 1 DP. The evaders may halt short of the full fast move distance once they are separated from enemy by friendly troops or a terrain obstacle. Skirmishers within 60 yds of friendly unit with pikes may 'take shelter' amongst the pikes if charged. In this case they move back behind the pikemen.

If the charger's opponent evades they must pursue (fast move unformed but without the 10 yd bonus) in an attempt to make contact. If they catch the evaders the evaders will be routed and the chargers get a free hack (see p.36). If the chargers encounter new enemy they will halt 20 yds short.

Failure to contact.

If the chargers fail to contact they they must take a control test the following turn even if under control. If they get other than an 'act as player wishes' result they must attempt to charge again.

Guns in Combat. Guns do not fight in hand to hand combat. If they are charged the gunners will abandon the guns and seek shelter with the nearest friendly troops. When guns are placed in front of enemy troops the charge moves through the guns (without disruption) to contact the troops behind. The fate of the gunners who sought shelter with friendly troops depends on the combat result. Guns without supporting troops within 40 yds are automatically overrun and the gunners assumed to have fled the field.

Combat Resolution. Opposing units determine the outcome of combat by rolling dice and comparing the *Hits* each have scored on the combat results table (see p.35).

Roll dice per base in contact (see next page) as follows:

    3 D6 for each front rank pike base standing to receive a cavalry charge.

    2 D6 for each front rank pike base charging or standing to receive a charge against others.

    1 D6 for all other bases and circumstances.

Then add or subtract additional dice for the following:

+2	A Grade (both types)
+1	B Grade
-1	D Grade
-2	E Grade
+1	leader inspiring (+1 for each inspire action, maximum +2)
+1	advantage of ground such as uphill or defending the edge of a town or wood
+1	cavalry or swordsmen charging
+1	additional if cavalry charging à l'outrance against other cavalry*
+1	pursuing or following-up
+1	additional if cavalry pursuing
+1	if supported (may not be combined with charging à l'outrance)
+1	cuirassiers fighting other cavalry
-1	each DP (maximum -5)
-2	infantry that moved this turn charged by cavalry**
-2	contacted in the flank or rear by a formed enemy charge originating from behind the flank or rear.

*In order to charge à l'outrance the unit must not have given fire that turn.

**This counts if the infantry moved in the movement or charge phase, although not if they only changed formation or facing.

Always roll at least 1 die even if the final tally is 0 or less.

A *Hit* is scored for each:

    6 if in column, unformed, if opponent defending fieldworks or fortifications, or if foot without pikes or fixed bayonets fighting cavalry*.

    5-6 in other circumstances.

*This counts if there are no pikes in the unit. It does not apply if the cavalry only contacted the shot armed bases of a mixed pike and shot unit as it is assumed that the shot will always be able to shelter amongst the pikes. It also does not count if the shot have fixed bayonets.

Compare difference of hits scored on the combat results chart (see p. 35)

Bases in combat.

Count all bases in direct base to base contact with enemy to their front, plus one base extending out on each flank for cavalry, swordsmen, rabble, pike-armed foot, and shot with fixed bayonets. Do not count *extending bases* of skirmishers or shot without fixed bayonets.

Pike-armed troops also count the bases in a second rank if charging or standing to receive a charge, as long as they are facing in good order and the rank in front is also pikemen.

Extending bases, second rank pikemen, and bases not facing their opponent, roll only 1 D6 per stand regardless of troop type.

Units that have been charged in the flank or rear do not count any extending or rear bases.

A double rank unit of horse counts as supported against its single rank opponent as long as it does not charge a l'outrance.

Supported.

A unit counts as *supported* if it has additional bases directly behind those in base to base contact, facing the enemy and in good order. This second line must have at least half as many bases as those in combat to count (ignoring shot in a unit of foot). The second line can be from the same or a different unit.

Skirmishers and shot cannot give support. Infantry cannot be supported by mounted nor mounted by infantry.

Units charging à l'outrance cannot count supported.

Multiple unit combat.

If two or more units on the same side are involved in a combat, average the grade of the bases in actual base to base contact (round up).

Use DPs of the unit in base to base contact with enemy that has the highest amount, ignore others.

Notes: Pikemen two ranks deep and facing their opponent will count the second rank if charging or standing to receive a charge. They will also count supported if the second rank has at least half as many pike bases as the front rank (ignoring shot).

Foot that moved in the movement phase are susceptible to disorder if charged by cavalry. Therefore the mere presence of cavalry may cause the foot to remain halted.

A furious combat between English and Spanish foot at a re-fight of the Battle of the Dunes

A unit of foot with shot extending out beyond the flanks of bases in contact will not count those extending bases unless they have fixed bayonets.

Combat Results

Compare the difference between the total Hits of each side:

+4 or more **Victory**	1 DP	Cavalry that charged only guns ride-through. Other A2, C, D and E Grade cavalry must pursue. Others take any permitted after combat action (see next page).
+1/+3 **Success**	1 DP	Cavalry that charged and failed to defeat formed foot (-3/-4 result), retire. Infantry facing cavalry remain in place. Cavalry that charged only guns ride-through. Others take any permitted after combat action.
Equal Result **Inconclusive**	2 DPs	Cavalry that charged foot retire. Infantry remain in place. Cavalry that charged à l'outrance against guns, unformed, or a single rank of enemy cavalry, ride-through. In other circumstances choose to remain in place or retire.
-1/-2 **Driven Back**	3 DPs	Infantry charged by cavalry only, remain in place. Other formed infantry fall back. Others retire (guns in this case, are abandoned but crew not killed).
-3/-4 **Defeat**	4 DPs	Guns abandoned and crew killed. Others *retire*.
-5 or more **Break**	5 DPs	Guns abandoned and crew killed. Others *rout*.

Spanish arquebusiers in pursuit. Units are automatically unformed when retiring or pursuing. A good way to show this is to space the bases apart to show the break up of the formation.

Actions Resulting from Combat.

Infantry 'taking the position' abandoned by their opponent.

After combat all units involved must take one of the actions listed below. These are conducted immediately with the losing unit moving first. In an inconclusive action where there is more than one one option, the player who had initiative decides last. The possible actions are:

Any permitted after combat action. Player may choose either to remain in place or to pursue an opponent that routed or retired. Cavalry may also choose to retire. Infantry may choose to take the position abandoned by retiring or routing enemy or to follow up enemy that fell back.

Remain in place. Take no action. If both sides remain in place then the combat continues the following turn.

Fall back. Move back one base depth facing the enemy.

Follow up. Move forward to remain in contact with an opponent that fell back.

Take the position. Move forward to occupy a position abandoned by retreating or routing enemy and remove 1 DP.

Ride-through. Move forwards, through the enemy position, a full 2 or 3 dice (player's option). End facing the nearest enemy threat and remove 1 DP. If there is no space for the ride-through either because the enemy are more than one rank deep or a supporting line is too close then the unit must either remain in place or retire. If a unit rides through and encounters new enemy or impassable terrain, it will halt beyond 20 yds.

Retire. Move back a full fast move, unformed, with maximum dice. Add 10 yds for each die rolled on the initial move only. They may halt short of the full move once behind other formed friends, fortifications or obstacle. Next turn they may either continue to retire unformed or remain in place to re-form back into line. Units unable to retire due to impassable terrain or enemy troops, remain in place and receive 1 DP. Retiring units caught by pursuers are automatically routed and the pursuers get a *free hack* (see below).

Rout. Move back a full fast move, unformed, with maximum dice until behind formed friendly foot or cavalry, or terrain obstacle, or 240 yds from enemy. Add 10 yds for each die rolled on the initial move only. Subsequent rout moves are made during opponent's move phase as long as the opponent is still pursuing in order to keep routers and pursuers moving together. A routing unit loses one casualty for each such subsequent rout move. If the routers outdistance pursuit and pass a control test with an *act as player wishes* result, they may rally and reform into line. Units unable to move due to impassable terrain or troops, remain in place and surrender to any enemy within 40 yds.

Pursue. Make a full fast move, unformed, in an attempt to remain in contact with opponents that evaded, retired or routed. Pursuers encountering new enemy immediately charge into them, the opponent may countercharge if cavalry. Pursuers that catch evading, routing or retiring units get an immediate *free hack*. If pursuers are not in contact with opponents they may reform if they pass a control test with an *act as player wishes* result.

Free Hack. This is worked out by rolling a D6 for every pursuing base in contact with retiring, or routing enemy, inflicting 1 casualty for every 4+ rolled.

Definitions

Advantage of Ground. A situation where a unit has an obvious terrain advantage over its opponent. This might be being uphill, behind an obstacle or defending the edge of a town or woods etc.

Any Permitted After Combat Action. A combat result in which the player may choose to remain in place or to pursue an opponent who routed or retired. Cavalry may also opt to retire and infantry may choose to take the position abandoned by retiring or routing enemy, or follow-up a fall-back.

Attached. A leader is attached if he is in base to base contact with a unit under his command. He moves with that unit and is bound by all fire and combat results. Attaching and detaching may only take place in the command phase. Only attached leaders may inspire or steady.

Base. A piece of card or similar material of standard size, mounting a group of figures.

Base to base contact. Normally this means the bases of each unit are in physical contact. However, for aesthetic reasons and to make it easier to distinguish between units, there may be a gap of up to 10 yds between units.

Breach. A gap in fortifications.

Battalia. A brigade of several units operating together under the leadership of a commander.

Casualty. A permanent reduction in a unit's strength by the removal of a base.

Cavalry. An inclusive term for cuirassiers, horse, light cavalry and mounted dragoons. It does not include dismounted dragoons.

Charge. A deliberate move intended to close to hand to hand combat with the enemy.

French foot level their pikes and make ready to charge.

Charge à l'outrance. Cavalry units closing with swords or lances without giving fire.

Column. Includes march and assault columns. March column is a marching formation only. Assault column is a special offensive formation adopted by foot to assault a breach in fortifications, to attack built up areas, or to move through rough terrain.

Cover. Terrain features such as woods and towns which restrict visibility. Hard Cover is that which also provides protection from fire such as solid barricades and fieldworks.

Control Test. A test that needs to be taken by units that are not under control.

Controlled Troops. Units that are being controlled by their leader and therefore do not need to take a control test.

DPs. Temporary death, disorder and desertion points used to record a unit's strength and morale.

Dragoons. Mounted infantry that will normally dismount to fight.

Evade. A move to avoid a charge.

Extending bases. Bases directly beside those in base to base contact facing enemy on either flank. They will be counted in combat (1 D6 regardless of troop type) if cavalry, swordsmen, rabble, pike-armed foot, or shot with fixed bayonets. Skirmishers and shot without fixed bayonets do not count.

Fieldworks. Battlefield earthworks, abatis and improvised barricades that provide a defensive barrier.

Flank. The side of a formed unit. To count as having been 'charged in the flank' the enemy charge must have originated from behind the flank.

Foot. Formed units of infantry with muskets and pikes. This does not include swordsmen, skirmishers, dismounted dragoons or rabble.

Free Hack. A quick calculation in which pursuers inflict casualties on routing, retiring or evading units they have contacted.

Halt. Remain in the same location but may fire and change formation or direction. A unit required to halt should be given a marker to remind players that it may not move normally.

Infantry. An inclusive term for foot, swordsmen, skirmishers and dismounted dragoons..

King James II of England at the Battle of the Boyne.

Battle is joined.

Leader. A generic term for all leaders: commanders and generals.

Light Troops. An inclusive term for skirmishers and light cavalry.

Line of Sight. A direct line from the unit in question to a specific point unblocked by intervening troops or terrain.

Morale DPs. These are DPs caused by retiring, routing, and destroyed friendly units or leaders. They cannot be removed by re-dressing ranks in the same turn that they were acquired.

Moves. There are 3 types: march move (beyond 120 yds of enemy), tactical move (within 120 yds), and charge move (to close into hand to hand combat).

Obstacles. Any linear structure or terrain feature which could impede movement, This includes rivers, streams, ditches, fortifications etc. Significant obstacles such as a fordable river can be classified as a *major obstacle*.

Orders. General instructions given to each battalia. Individual units do not require orders.

Re-dress ranks. The removal of DPs by a unit that is not in combat and took no DPs from artillery fire this turn. The number of DPs and the circumstances that may be removed is dependent on the unit's efficiency grade.

Stationary. This means not moving and not changing formation or direction. It does not preclude firing.

Take the Position. An option open to foot in some circumstances after combat. It allows the unit to advance to occupy a position abandoned by retiring or routing enemy.

Under Control. Units that have an attached leader or are within 60 yds of a detached leader (+40 yds for each additional leader action), are considered to be under control and will not need to take a control test other than to stop rout, pursuit or charge.

Unit. A tactical group operating as a single entity.

Close Fire & European Order XVII — Quick Reference

Sequence of Play

Bombardment. Guns may fire or reserve shot.

Musketry. Foot may fire or fix/unfix bayonets. May not move if they fire. Cavalry and skirmishers may not fire.

Command. Command actions and control tests.

Movement. Move units. Must halt at 20 yds from enemy.

Close Fire. Guns that reserved shot may fire out to 120 yds. Cavalry and infantry may fire at any range even if moved.

Combat. In the following order: declare and execute charges and responses; resolve all hand to hand combat; conduct any resulting moves

Morale. Redress ranks. Assign DPs for morale.

Move Distances

Guns may not move once unlimbered except light guns may make a march move at infantry speed.

March Move. Starts and ends beyond 120 yds of enemy. Infantry up to 160 yds, cavalry up to 240 yds. Infantry up to 240 yds if march column on road.

Tactical Move (within 120 yds of enemy):
- Infantry: 1 AvD + 1 optional D6 x 10yds.
- Cavalry: 1 or 2 AvD + 1 optional D6 x 10yds.
- Inspired unit: +10 yds for each die rolled.
- Road move: up to 120 yds if in march column. No dice required. Negates effect of rough terrain.

Fast Move (evade, rout, retire and pursuit):
Maximum dice and all optional additions. +10 yds for each die rolled on initial rout, evade or retire move (not pursuit).

Detached leaders/messengers: up to 120 yds (240 if beyond 120 yds of enemy.

Fatigue and Disorder: No penalty if march column, unformed, or limbered guns. Otherwise:
- *Good terrain.* 6 rolled on move die = 1 DP if in line. No penalty if in assault column.
- *Rough terrain.* 5-6 = 1 DP if in line. 4 = 1 additional DP if cavalry. Assault column take 1 DP on 6 only.

Morale DPs

General killed or routing in 120 yds = 2 DPs
Commander killed or routing in 120 yds = 1 DP
Equal or higher routing or destroyed in 120 yds = 2 DPs
Lower grade routing or destroyed in 120 yds = 1 DP
Equal or higher grade foot retiring in 120 yds = 1 DP
Evade = 1 DP
Ride through or take the position after combat = -1DP

Redress Ranks

Remove DPs if not in combat and no DPs from artillery fire:

A1 Grade. -1 DP & 1 additional if if stationary.
A2, B & C Grade. -1 DP if stationary.
D & E Grade. -1 DP if stationary and not under fire.

Command Actions

Move up to 120 yds; attach and/or detach.

Issue or listen to new orders.

Influence unit to which he is attached:
  Steady - remove 1 DP. Unit must remain halted.
  Inspire - increase combat effectiveness and move speed.

Control Test

Take if beyond 60 yds of detached leader (+40 yds for each additional leader action) unless:
- unit with attached leader.
- part of a continuous line with controlled unit of the same battalia and will conform to its movement.
- within 60 yds, behind a controlled unit of the same battalia, and will conform to movement of the lead unit.

Must always test if charged last turn and failed to contact or wishing cease rout, pursuit, or looting, even if under control.

Roll 1 D6:
+ or -1 (optional) if leader attached.
+ or -1 (optional) if guns or A1 or B Grade.

Results.
Continue rout/pursuit/loot/charge unless 3-4 result. Otherwise:
  2- = Halt.
  3-4 = Act as player wishes.
  5+ = Repeat last move.

Manoeuvre

Wheel: 1 DP in 120 yds of enemy. No penalty column or unformed.

Change Formation. 1 move and 1 DP if within 120 yds of enemy. ½ move, no DP if further away.

Re-form: 1 move, once cause ceased.

Unlimber: 1 move and 1 DP (2 DPs if under fire).

Cross major obstacle: ½ move, 1 DP (2 if under fire).

Cross minor obstacle: count as rough terrain.

About face: ½ move, 1 DP if cavalry within 120 yds of enemy or if foot under fire.

Incline: A-B Grade foot only. Equal forwards and sideways.

Side-step/step-back 20 yds: A-B Grade foot only.

Mount/Dismount: ½ move, 1 DP if under fire.

Pass a gap: 1 DP if within 120 yds of enemy. Reduce foot move by ½, or change into column.

Passage of Lines: No penalty if passing through guns. Otherwise no penalty if none routing, one is stationary, did not fire. Otherwise 1 DP on each formed unit.

Maximum DPs. Once a unit has 3 DPs for any reason it no longer incurs any more DPs for movement or manoeuvre.

Risk to Leader.

Roll one D6: 1= Hit. Roll again:
  1 = Killed
  2-4 = Wounded. Loose 1 action. Killed on 2nd wound.
  5-6 = Near miss. No effect

Ranges

	Maximum Range	Effective Range	Close Range
Heavy Gun	720 yds	360 yds	120 yds
Med/Lt Gun	480 yds	240 yds	120 yds
Musketry	120 yds	-	40 yds
Cavalry	40 yds	-	40 yds

Artillery Fire. Roll 1 D6 per gun. Modified as follows:

Same target and range	+1	New target	-1
Column or enfilade	+1	Each DP	-1
Beyond effective range	-1	Target in fieldworks	-1
Heavy Gun	+1	Light Gun	-1

Results:
    Beyond close range: 4+ = 1 DP on target
    Close range: 2-3 = 1 DP, 4+ = 2 DPs

Infantry and Cavalry Fire:
1 D6 per base -DPs on unit firing.
Halve dice if target in fieldworks or hard cover. Round up.

Result:
5-6 = 1 DP on target if formed foot firing at close range.
6 = 1 DP on target in other circumstances.

Combat and Close Fire
Roll dice for each base in contact as follows:
3 D6 for each front rank pike receiving cavalry charge.
2 D6 for each front rank pike base in other charge combats.
1 D6 per base in other circumstances.
+2 if A Grade; +1 if B Grade
-1 if D Grade; -2 if E Grade
+1 leader inspiring (+1 each action to max +2)
+1 advantage of ground
+1 cavalry or swordsmen charging,
+1 additional if charging à l'outrance vs. cavalry
+1 following-up or pursuing
+1 additional if cavalry pursuing
+1 if cuirassiers fighting other cavalry
+1 if supported unless charging à l'outrance
-1 for each DP (maximum -5)
-2 if infantry that moved charged by cavalry
-2 if hit in flank/rear by charge from behind flank/rear

+1 D6 per eligible extending base extending on either flank.
Pikemen +1 D6 per second rank base in charge combat only.

A Hit is scored for each:
- 6 if in column or unformed, if opponent defending fieldworks, or infantry with no pikes or fixed bayonets fighting cavalry.
- 5-6 in other circumstances.

Combat Results. Compare Hits:

4+ Victory	1 DP	Cavalry that charged only guns ride-through. Other A2, C, D and E Grade cavalry must pursue. Others take any permitted after combat action.
+1/3 Success	1 DP	Cavalry retire if charged and failed to defeat foot. Infantry facing cavalry remain in place. Cavalry that charged only guns ride-through. Others take any permitted after combat action.
Equal result Inconclusive	2 DPs each	Cavalry that charged foot retire. Infantry remain in place. Cavalry that charged à l'outrance against guns, unformed, or a single rank of enemy cavalry, ride-through. In other circumstances choose to remain in place or retire.
-1/-2 Driven Back	3 DPs	Infantry charged by cavalry only, remain in place. Other formed infantry fall back. Guns abandoned but crew not killed. Others retire.
-3/-4 Defeat	4 DPs	Guns abandoned and crew killed. Others retire.
-8 Break	5 DPs	Guns abandoned and crew killed. Others rout.

Movement after Combat

Any permitted action. May choose to remain in place or pursue. Cavalry may also retire, and foot may take the position abandoned by retiring enemy or follow-up a fall-back.

Remain in place. Take no action. If both sides remain in place then the combat continues the following turn.

Fall-back and follow-up. Fall back one base depth facing enemy. Follow-up to remain in contact with fall-back.

Ride-through. Move 2 or 3 dice (player's option) through the enemy position. End facing the nearest threat. If the unit encounters new enemy or impassable terrain, it will halt beyond 20 yds. Remove 1 DP.

Take the position. Move forward to occupy an abandoned position. Remove 1 DP.

Retire. Move back a full fast unformed move. May halt short once behind other formed friends or obstacle. Next turn may either continue to retire or remain in place to reform. If unable to retire, remain in place and receive 1 DP. Break if caught by pursuers and the pursuers get a *free hack.*

Rout. Full fast unformed move, until behind formed friends, or obstacle, or 240 yds from enemy. Then may take a control test to attempt to stop rout, succeeding on *act as player wishes* result.

Pursue. Full fast unformed move, in an attempt to remain in contact with opponents who retired or routed. Pursuers encountering new enemy charge. Pursuers who catch routing or retiring units get a *free hack.*

Free Hack. Roll 1 D6 for every pursuing base in contact, inflicting 1 casualty for every 4+ rolled.